TIME TRAVEL GUIDES

THE AZTEC EMPIRE

EXPRESS EDITION

Jane Bingham

www.raintree.co.uk/library
Visit our website to find out more information

To order:
☎ Phone 44 (0) 1865 888112
🖷 Send a fax to 44 (0) 1865 314091
🖳 Visit the Raintree bookshop at www.raintree.co
order online.

First published in Great Britain by Raintree, Halley Court,
Jordan Hill, Oxford OX2 8EJ, part of Harcourt Education.
Raintree is a registered trademark of Harcourt Education
Ltd.

© Harcourt Education Ltd 2008
First published in paperback in 2008
The moral right of the proprietor has been asserted.

Editorial: Sarah Shannon, Lucy Beevor,
    and Harriet Milles
Adaptation for Freestyle Express: Sarah Levete
    and Geoff Barker
Design: Steve Mead, Geoff Ward, and Ian Winton
Picture Research: Erica Newbery
Illustrations: Eikon Illustration & Tim Slade
Production: Duncan Gilbert

Originated by Modern Age
Printed and bound in China by South China
    Printing Company Limited

ISBN 978 1 4062 0862 7 (hardback)
12 11 10 09 08
10 9 8 7 6 5 4 3 2 1

ISBN 978 1 4062 0869 6 (paperback)
12 11 10 09 08
10 9 8 7 6 5 4 3 2 1

British Library Cataloguing in Publication Data
Bingham, Jane
The Aztec empire. - (Time travel guides)
1. Aztecs - Juvenile literature
972'.018
A full catalogue record for this book is available from the
British Library.

Acknowledgements
The publishers would like to thank the following for
permission to reproduce photographs:
AKG Images **pp. 13, 14, 27, 48**; Alamy **pp. 36** (Nature
Picture Library), **41** (Visual Arts Library), **43** (World
Pictures Ltd.), **46** (Gary Cook); Art Archive **pp. 24–25, 26,
32–33** (Museo Ciudad, Mexico/Dagli Orti), **39, 50–51,
53** (Museo del Templo Mayor, Mexico/Dagli Orti),
49 (Museum für Völkerkunde, Vienna/Dagli Orti), **21**
(National Anthropological Museum, Mexico City/Dagli
Orti), **8, 37, 38–39, 44–45** (National Palace, Mexico
City/Dagli Orti), **22, 35** (Templo Mayor Library, Mexico/
Dagli Orti), **29** (Dagli Orti), **54–55** (Nicolas Sapieha),
16, 18, 19, 21, 30, 47, 52; Bridgeman **pp. 56–57**; Corbis
p. 31 (Macduff Everton); Digital Vision **p. 10**; Getty
Images **pp. 12** (The Image Bank/Gabriel M Covian), **6–7**
(National Geographic/Stephen Alvarez); NHPA **p. 30**
(Kevin Schafer); Scala Archives/British Museum, London
p. 23.

Cover photograph of an Aztec pyramid reproduced with
permission of Alamy Images/Hugh Taylor. Photograph
of the Stone of the Sun reproduced with permission of
Ancient Art & Architecture Collection Ltd/ Dr.S.Coyne.
Photograph of an ornament in the form of a double-
headed serpent reproduced with permission of the
Werner Forman Archive/British Museum, London.

The publishers would like to thank Paul Steele for his
assistance in the preparation of this book.

Every effort has been made to contact copyright holders
of any material reproduced in this book. Any omissions
will be rectified in subsequent printings if notice is given
to the publishers.

CONTENTS

Words that appear in the text in bold, **like this**, are explained in the Glossary.

VALLEY OF MEXICO

OF GULF OF MEXICO

N
W E
S

Tuxpan

Tula

Teotihuacán

Lake Texcoco

Tenochtitlán

TENOCHTITLÁN

TWIN VOLCANOES
POPOCATÉPETL &
IXTACÍHUATL

Oaxaca

PACIFIC OCEAN

Mexico

Gulf of Mexico

Pacific Ocean

Central America

South America

☐ AZTEC EMPIRE

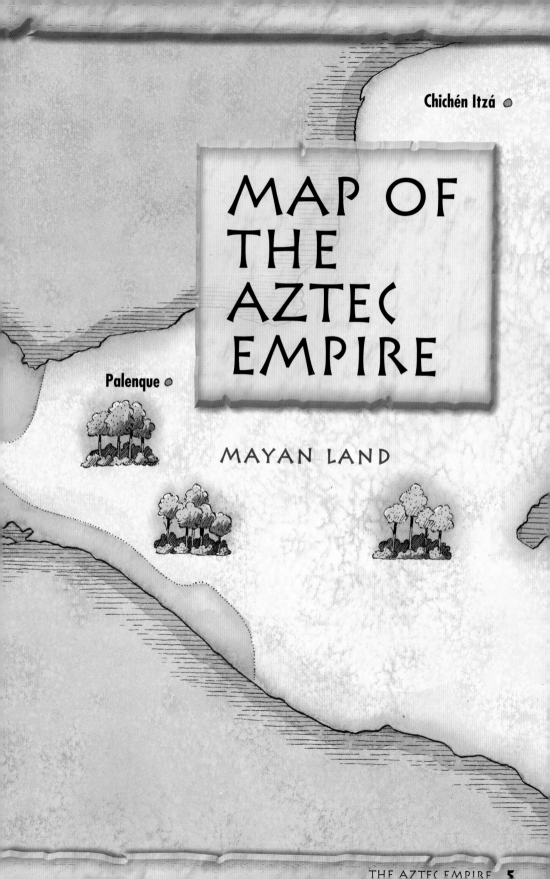

MAP OF THE AZTEC EMPIRE

Chichén Itzá

Palenque

MAYAN LAND

The Aztec Empire is a dangerous place. But this guide (and a bit of luck) will help you stay safe.

CHAPTER 1

FACTS ABOUT THE AZTEC EMPIRE

You are about to go on an exciting holiday. You are travelling to the Aztec **Empire**. An empire is land under the control of a leader. You will pass through rainforests. Here you will see amazing wildlife. You can climb high mountains. Or you can walk around Tenochtitlán. This is a beautiful city on a lake. There's lots to do here. Enjoy your trip!

WHEN TO TRAVEL

The Aztec **civilization** began around AD 1150. That was nearly 900 years ago. A civilization is a society or group of people living at a particular time. The Aztec civilization lasted for four hundred years.

By 1325 the Aztecs will have settled by Lake Texcoco. They will be building the city of Tenochtitlán. This is a city on a lake.

BUILDING AN EMPIRE

The Aztecs worked hard to build up their **empire**. An empire is land under the control of one leader. The Aztecs fought other **tribes** (groups of people). They took land from these tribes.

The best time to visit is around 1510. You will find an empire of about six million people. The ruler is a powerful **emperor**.

This is a modern painting. It shows how the city of Tenochtitlán may have looked in the 1500s.

↰ This picture shows insects called locusts. They are attacking the Aztecs' crops (food).

TIMES TO AVOID

Plan your visit carefully. Avoid times when there is a **famine**. There is not enough food to eat at these times.

Don't visit the Aztec Empire after 1519. Hernán Cortés arrives then from the country of Spain. He brings his army. Cortés and his men destroy most of the Aztecs' buildings. By 1521 the mighty Aztec Empire is in ruins.

GOOD AND BAD TIMES

AD 1325	The Aztecs settle along Lake Texcoco
1400s	The Aztecs start building their empire
1446	Insects called locusts attack crops
1450–1454	Famine
1490–1500	The Aztec Empire is very powerful
1500	Floods in Tenochtitlán
1505	Famine
1508–1518	The Aztec Empire is at its largest
1519	Spanish troops arrive
1520	Disease called smallpox spreads through the empire
1521	The Aztec Empire is destroyed

The best time to visit is 1490–1500 or 1508–1518.

LAND AND WEATHER

The Aztec **Empire** stretches from the Gulf of Mexico to the Pacific Ocean (see map on page 4). It measures around 280,000 square kilometres (108,000 square miles). The empire covers many types of land.

WET AND MUDDY

Near the sea, there are a few small fishing villages. Not much happens in the villages. As you go inland, you can see farmers. They work in the fields. This area is flat. It is wet and muddy.

Rainforest trees tower over the centre of the empire.

RAINFOREST

There's a large area of rainforest in the heart of the empire. You can see mountains. There are rivers and large lakes. This is where most cities are.

A local guide will help you through the thick rainforest. You can only reach some towns by crossing dangerous mountain passes.

WATCH THE WEATHER

Be ready for lots of different weather. In the rainforests it is hot and steamy. In the mountains it can be freezing.

From June to October is the rainy season. There are heavy rains. The land floods. But watch out too for long periods of **drought**. There is no rain. The crops dry up and die in the fields.

FARMING

The Aztecs grow vegetables such as beans and maize. Maize is a type of corn. They also grow fruit and flowers.

Some farmers grow crops in fields in the mountains. The fields are cut into the side of the mountain. They look like steps. Others farm on floating fields. These are in the middle of Lake Texcoco.

NATURAL RICHES

The Aztecs **mine** (dig) the mountains for gold, silver, and copper. They also mine for precious stones such as jade.

EXPLODING MOUNTAINS!

You will see **volcanoes** like the ones in the picture. Volcanoes are mountains. They sometimes explode with hot rock.

WHO'S WHO IN THE AZTEC EMPIRE?

Aztec society is very organized. It is important to know where everyone belongs.

- The **emperor** is at the top of Aztec society. He is treated like a god. He makes all the important decisions.
- Next come people called nobles. Some nobles are priests. Others are leaders of the army.
- Beneath the nobles are soldiers.
- Next come ordinary people called **commoners**. They can be farmers or **craftworkers**. Craftworkers make things such as jewellery.
- Slaves are at the bottom of Aztec society. They are often killed as gifts for the gods.

MUTECZUMA

Rex ultimus Mexicanorum

Emperors, such as Moctezuma II (pictured) rule the **empire**.

COUNCILS

Nobles are important people. They meet in groups called councils. The councils advise the **emperor** (ruler).

CLANS

Small areas of the empire are divided into groups. These are called **clans**. Each clan is made up of about 200 families. Each clan is run by a group of leaders. They are responsible for the clan's farms and markets. They are responsible for the clan's schools.

The men in each clan have to do something for the emperor. Some fight in the army. Others help to build palaces.

Aztec nobles offer gifts to a corn goddess. >

CONQUERED TRIBES

The Aztecs conquer (take over) other **tribes** or groups. Each tribe must give something to the emperor. This is called a **tribute**. Tributes can include animals or birds. They can include honey or gold.

AZTEC CLOTHES

The Aztecs have strict rules about what people wear. Anyone who breaks the rules can be put to death. So make sure you dress properly!

- Emperor and nobles wear clothes made from cotton.
- Others wear clothes made from rougher material.
- Nobles wear sandals. They go barefoot when they are in the presence of the emperor.
- **Commoners** (ordinary people) go barefoot.
- Nobles can wear golden jewellery.
- Commoners' jewellery is made from shells or stones.

CLOTHES FOR COMMONERS

Male **commoners** (ordinary people) wear knee-length pieces of material. These are called tunics. They are tied at the shoulder. Women wear loose tops and simple skirts.

High up in the mountains, people wear blankets. They knot them round their necks to keep warm. During the cold night, the blankets are used as bedding.

Men working in the fields wrap material around their bodies.

KEEPING CLEAN

The Aztecs like to keep clean. Most families have a bathhouse outside their home. The family lights a fire outside the bathhouse. The bathhouse has mud walls. The fire makes the mud walls really hot. The family goes inside. They throw water against the walls. This makes hot steam. This helps them get really clean.

NOBLE DRESS

Aztec nobles love to dress up. They wear long cotton cloaks. These are decorated with jewels and gold thread. The finest cloaks are made from coloured feathers. Nobles wear lots of jewellery.

Nobles wear jewellery such as armbands and necklaces. They also wear jewellery in their lips, nose, and ears.

...LIFE

...u do as you're told in the land of the
... children learn to obey their parents.
Anyone who disobeys faces some nasty punishments.

LESSONS AT HOME

Aztec children help their parents. The children of
farmers work in the fields. Young **craftworkers** are
taught skills. Then they can help their fathers. Boys
are also taught to hunt and fish.

CHILDREN BEWARE!

These pictures show some Aztec punishments. Someone holds a child over a hot
fire (top right). The fire is made from chilli peppers. The smoke makes the child's
eyes sting badly. Someone pricks a child with spikes from a cactus plant. The child
is left in a puddle for a day (bottom right).

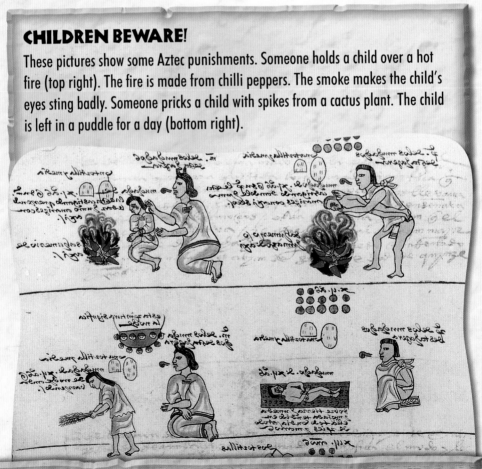

Most 12 year-old girls know how to grind up maize (corn). This turns it into flour. They make bread with the flour.

AZTEC SCHOOLS

Most Aztec children go to a "youth house". Here priests teach them about their history and religion. Boys learn building and fighting skills. Girls learn how to be good housekeepers.

The sons of noble families attend a special school. Here they can train to be priests. They can also train to be leaders of the army.

TIME TO MARRY

Aztec girls usually marry between the ages of 12 to 15. Boys marry in their late teens.

Husbands earn enough money to support their families. Wives have to run the home. They have to obey their husbands.

WORDS, NUMBERS, AND TIME

PICTURE WRITING

Aztecs don't write words. Instead, they use picture symbols. These are called **glyphs**. Glyphs can show an object. They can also show a creature, or a person. Sometimes a glyph is a simple sign. For example, the Aztec sign for a journey is a set of footprints. The sign for war is a shield and arrows.

Lizard

The Aztecs show a number with dots. The number seven is usually shown as a pattern of seven dots.

Snake

FOLDED BOOKS

Aztec books are made from strips of bark. They are sometimes made from deer skin. The books fold up like a fan. This book is called a **codex**.

AZTEC CALENDARS

Aztecs use two different calendars. Priests use one calendar. It helps them work out when to hold their festivals. Ordinary people use the other calendar. It helps them work out important dates, such as market days.

caption to follow caption to follow caption here caption to follow here caption to follow here

↖ This is a picture of the Stone of the Sun or Calendar Stone. It shows Aztec days, months, and years.

Check which calendar an Aztec is using. It can be very confusing.

AZTEC RELIGION

The Aztecs believe that gods control everything. There are different gods for different things (see box on page 23). You will see places called **shrines**. You will see places called **temples**. These places are built for the gods.

The Aztecs try to keep their gods happy by offering **sacrifices**. These are gifts of specially killed humans. Animals are also killed as sacrifices.

GIFTS FOR THE GODS

Humans are killed as sacrifices. Their hearts are ripped out. These may be a gift for the gods.

WATCH OUT!
The Aztecs sometimes kill foreigners (people from other countries). They give their bodies to the god Huitzilopochtli as a gift!

HVITZILOPOCHTLI

Huitzilopochtli is the special god of the Aztec rulers. He is the god of war. There is a shrine to him on top of the Great Temple in Tenochtitlán. Each evening, Aztecs kill prisoners. They give the prisoners' hearts as gifts to Huitzilopochtli. Then they throw the bodies down the temple steps.

Human sacrifices have to wear masks like this.

ANIMAL GODS

Many Aztec gods have links with animals. Huitzilopochtli is sometimes known as the Hummingbird.

GODS AND GODDESSES AT A GLANCE

- **Huitzilopochtli** – special god of the Aztec rulers.
- **Quetzalcoatl** – god of creation (maker of things).
- **Tlaloc** – god of rain and lightning.
- **Coatlicue** – goddess of the Earth.
- **Coyolxauhqui** – goddess of the Moon.
- **Tonatiuh** – god of the Sun.
- **Mictlantecuhtli** – god of death.

This is a modern painting of Tenochtitlán.

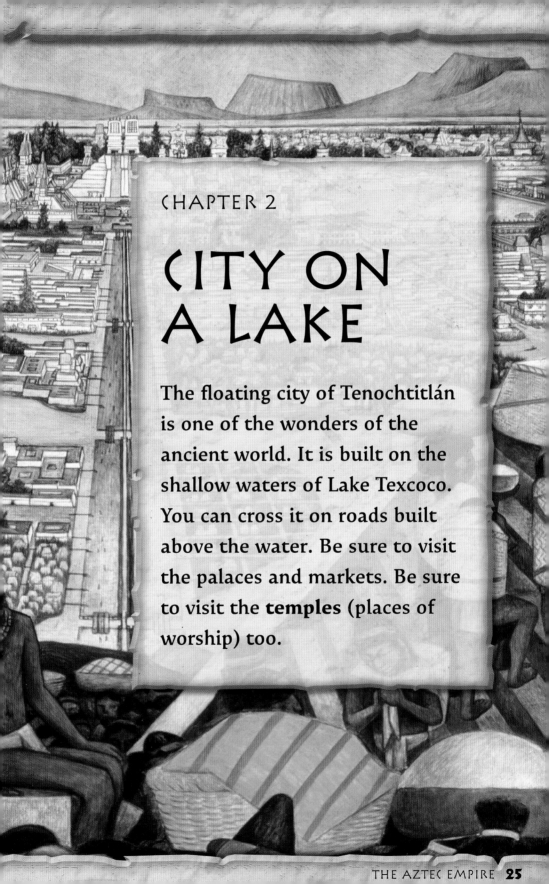

CHAPTER 2

CITY ON A LAKE

The floating city of Tenochtitlán is one of the wonders of the ancient world. It is built on the shallow waters of Lake Texcoco. You can cross it on roads built above the water. Be sure to visit the palaces and markets. Be sure to visit the **temples** (places of worship) too.

THE STORY OF TENOCHTITLÁN

In the 12th century, the Aztecs left northern Mexico. That is over 900 years ago. They travelled south. They wanted land to grow crops. Around 1325, they settled by Lake Texcoco. The Aztecs built islands. They made them from plants and mud. This was the start of the city of Tenochtitlán.

THE EAGLE AND THE CACTUS

The Aztecs believe they saw a sign from the gods at Lake Texcoco. They saw a white eagle on a cactus. It had a snake in its claws. This sign meant the Aztecs should settle here. In Aztec picture language, the eagle on the cactus is the sign for Tenochtitlán.

A GROWING CITY

The Aztecs built raised roads called **causeways**. These linked the islands to the **mainland**. The mainland is the main part of the country. The city of Tenochtitlán was divided into four areas around a square. The square was used for religious occasions.

BRILLIANT BUILDINGS

Emperor Moctezuma I built a pyramid to the god Huitzilopochtli. A pyramid is a tall triangle-shaped building. The emperor also built a royal palace. It had beautiful gardens.

THE END OF TENOCHTITLÁN

In 1519, Hernán Cortés arrived in Tenochtitlán. He came with his army from the country of Spain. Cortés and his men found a beautiful city. But two years later they destroyed the city. This was the end of Tenochtitlán. Cortés began building a new city. This was the start of the modern Mexico City.

This picture shows the Spanish arriving in Mexico in 1519.

EXPLORING TENOCHTITLÁN

There is a large square in Tenochtitlán. This is where all the major religious **ceremonies** (events) are held. **Commoners** (ordinary people) are not allowed here. Wear your noble clothes if you want to look around.

THE GREAT TEMPLE

Make sure you visit the Great **Temple**. This is the tallest and grandest building in the land. It measures 27 metres tall. There is a steep flight of steps leading to the top.

On top of the temple are two **shrines**. These are for the gods Tlaloc and Huitzilopochtli. Shrines are places where you can worship.

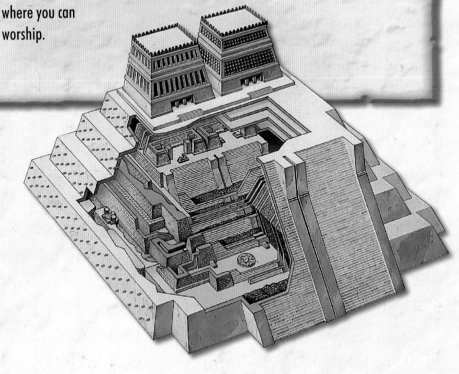

INSIDE THE GREAT TEMPLE

Inside the Great **Temple** the Aztecs leave offerings to the gods. The temple is filled with precious gifts. The gifts include masks and necklaces.

SKULL RACK

Near the Great Temple is a large building. It is built from human skulls (heads). They are the skulls of people who were killed for the gods! This photo shows a copy of the original skull rack.

DOWN THE STEPS

At the base of the Great Temple there is a large stone. It is carved with a picture of the Moon goddess. Her name is Coyolxauhqui. The Aztecs believe that she fought with her brother, the Sun god, on a mountaintop. His name is Huitzilopochtli. He won the fight. He chopped up his sister's body. He threw it down the mountain. This is why Aztecs throw bodies down the Great Temple steps after killing them (see page 23).

MORE CITY SIGHTS

There are more than four palaces to explore in Tenochtitlán. Each one has beautiful gardens. There are fountains in the gardens. The palace of **Emperor** (ruler) Moctezuma II even has its own private zoo!

MOCTEZUMA'S ZOO

If you like birds, head for Emperor Moctezuma's zoo. The Emperor has ten different bird pools in his gardens. Some are homes for river birds. Others are filled with saltwater. These are for seabirds.

The Aztecs believe the quetzal bird is sacred (holy). Emperors and priests wear the birds' feathers in their clothes.

ROYAL PALACES

Each palace is like a small town. It has hundreds of rooms and thousands of slaves. There's a grand throne room, guest rooms, and meeting halls. There are libraries and storerooms. There are dungeons for prisoners. Make sure you've got plenty of energy to visit. It takes a long time to walk around!

HOLY BALL

Remember to visit the **sacred** ball court. You might see a game of *tlachtli*. Two teams play this sacred game. It stands for the battle between life and death. It can be dangerous to join in. The winning team is killed for the gods!

ANCIENT GAME

In *tlachtli* players try to hit a rubber ball. They shoot the ball through a stone hoop. This is set high on a wall (right). The players hit the ball with their arms and knees. The players wear arm and knee pads. They also wear leather helmets.

This picture shows Aztecs marching towards the Valley of Mexico.

CHAPTER 3

TRAVEL, FOOD, AND SHELTER

In the Aztec **Empire** (land), you will travel either on foot or in a canoe. There are no wheeled vehicles. There are no animals to carry loads or people. But it's worth the effort to travel around. You'll see mountains, forests, and beaches. Along the way, eat some tasty meals.

ON THE MOVE

Walk barefoot if you are travelling with ordinary **commoners**. You might find a slave to carry your luggage though.

TRAVEL BY CANOE

It's best to travel by canoe. There are many lakes. There are also many rivers and canals.

The Aztecs use flat-bottomed canoes. They carve them out of tree trunks. The canoes are quite difficult to use. Ask an Aztec to paddle you around.

Town houses usually have flat roofs.

PLACES TO STAY

There are no hotels in the Aztec Empire. You need to stay with local people. But make sure you are well behaved. The Aztecs often **sacrifice** (kill) visitors from other countries. They give them as gifts to their gods!

Aztec homes are made from mud bricks. They have very few windows. This means they stay cool inside. Furniture is simple. There are **reed** (grass) mats on the floor. Benches and tables are made from reeds.

Houses in the country have roofs made from reeds. City houses usually have a flat roof. There is only a ground floor. Only nobles and emperors can build houses of more than two levels.

These Aztec women prepare a feast.

City houses are grouped around a courtyard. Several families share the courtyard. This is where the women work. They prepare and cook meals.

FOOD AND DRINK

Most meals include a tortilla. This is a type of flat pancake. It is made from maize (see box below). The Aztecs wrap the tortilla around different fillings. There is plenty of fresh food for fillings.

LOTS OF CORN

Maize is a vegetable. It is also called corn. It grows all over the Aztec **Empire** (land). You can eat it as corn on the cob. Usually it is dried. Then it is ground into flour. This is used to make tortillas.

FRESH VEG

There are lots of vegetables to eat. These include peppers and tomatoes. There are also leeks, watercress, and artichokes. Aztecs cook vegetables with onions and garlic. But watch out. The Aztecs put chilli peppers in almost everything! Chillies are spicy vegetables. They make the food taste hot and spicy.

MEAT, FISH, AND OTHER TREATS

Aztecs fish and hunt. They catch duck, turkey, and deer. They also eat parrots, owls, eagles, and frogs. Birds' and insects' eggs are a great treat.

VERY HOT CHOCOLATE

Aztec **emperors** (rulers) like to end the day with a drink of hot chocolate. But this is hot chocolate with a difference. It is made from **cacao beans** (cocoa beans). It also has vanilla, spices, and chilli in it. It's hot and spicy!

If you are offered a chocolate drink, you are very special. The Aztecs think that chocolate is the drink of the gods. **Commoners** (ordinary people) are not allowed to try it!

The Aztecs use cacao beans to make chocolate. They also use the beans as money.

The **emperor** (ruler) accepts gifts. He is dressed in the blue feather headdress.

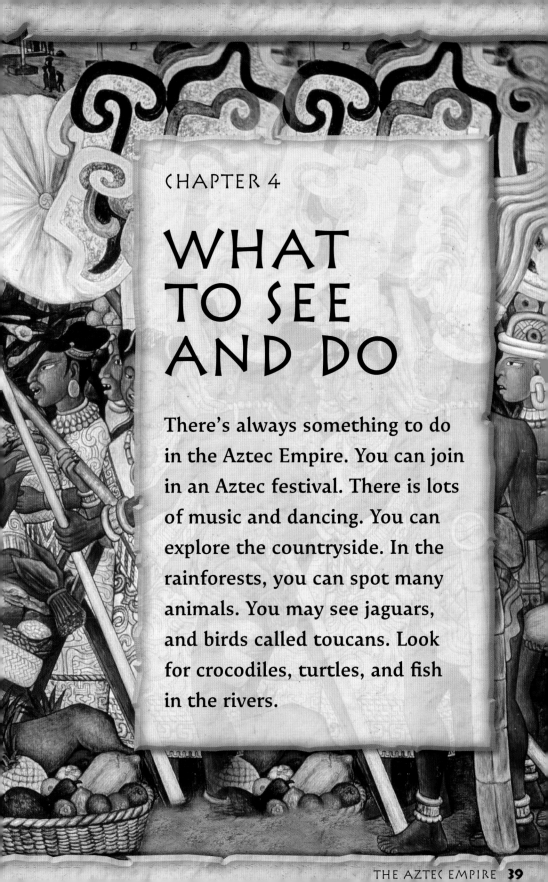

CHAPTER 4

WHAT TO SEE AND DO

There's always something to do in the Aztec Empire. You can join in an Aztec festival. There is lots of music and dancing. You can explore the countryside. In the rainforests, you can spot many animals. You may see jaguars, and birds called toucans. Look for crocodiles, turtles, and fish in the rivers.

CEREMONIES AND FESTIVALS

The Aztecs love putting on a show. But watch out. Some celebrations are quite violent!

SPRING FESTIVALS

In spring, there is a celebration for Xipe Totec, the god of Spring. Farmers dance to encourage the corn to grow. Look carefully at the dancers' cloaks. They are made from human skin. These people were **sacrifices**. They were killed as gifts for the gods.

AZTEC WEDDINGS

The bride's face is painted with yellow paint. Her arms and legs are covered in red feathers. The couple sprinkle **incense** over each other. This smells sweet. Then the bridegroom's cloak is tied to the bride's clothes. This is a sign that they are married.

NEW FIRE CEREMONY

The New Fire **Ceremony** takes place every 52 years. To take part, you need to visit in the years 1403, 1455, or 1507.

In the ceremony, 52 wooden rods are tied together. This marks the end of 52 years. Then people light a "new fire". This marks the start of the next 52 years.

Before the New Fire ceremony, people fear that the world will end. For twelve days no one lights a fire. People only eat bread and water. At midnight on the twelfth day a fire is lit. When the Sun rises in the morning they celebrate for days.

WAR OF FLOWERS!

Sometimes the Aztecs run out of human **sacrifices** (people killed as gifts for the gods). Then, two armies of knights fight each other. The losers are sacrificed. The battle is called the War of Flowers. This is because of the knights' colourful costumes. When they fight, they look like flowers.

LOOKING AT HISTORY

Explore the history of the area. There were several important **civilizations** (societies) before the Aztecs. The Aztecs copied some of their traditions (ways of doing things).

THE CITY OF TEOTIHUACÁN

Teotihuacán is the biggest ancient city in Central America. The earlier settlers began building it around 100 BC. That is over 2,000 years ago. At the centre of the city were two **temples**. These are places for the gods. They are called the Pyramid of the Sun and the Pyramid of the Moon.

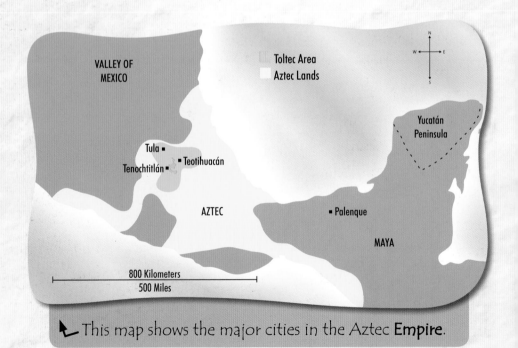

This map shows the major cities in the Aztec **Empire**.

MAYA

The Mayan civilization began about 3,500 years ago (around 1500 BC). This was in the Yucatan **peninsula** (see map on page 42). This piece of land sticks out into the sea. Later the Maya people began building cities in many parts of Mexico. This happened nearly 1,750 years later.

You can explore the remains of the great Mayan city at Palenque. There are many beautiful temples. There is also a building for studying the stars. By the 900s, the great Mayan cities were deserted. That was over 1,100 years ago.

TOLTECS

The Toltecs were **warriors** (fighters). They were also **craftworkers** (people with skills). About 1,000 years ago, the Toltecs built a great city at Tula. Other **tribes** or groups of people finally forced the Toltecs out of Mexico.

These are giant statues of Toltec warriors.

This modern painting shows market day in Tenochtitlán.

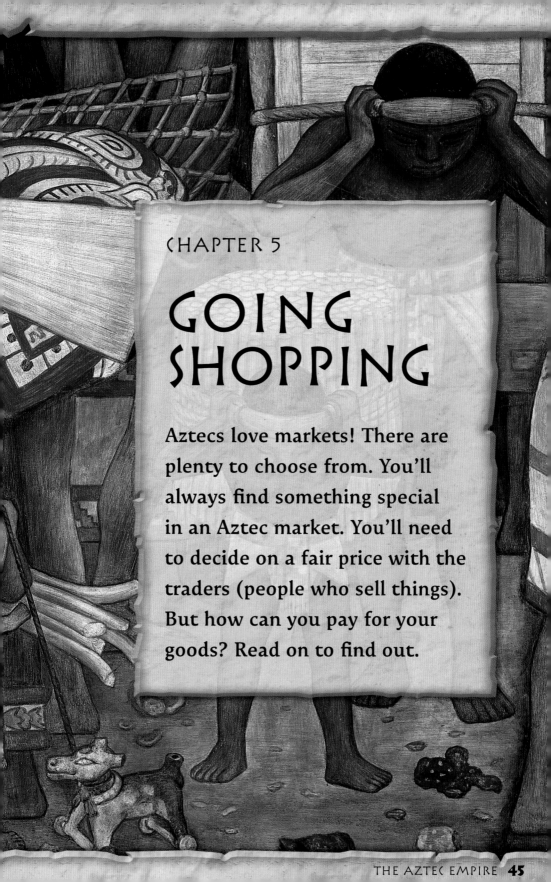

CHAPTER 5

GOING SHOPPING

Aztecs love markets! There are plenty to choose from. You'll always find something special in an Aztec market. You'll need to decide on a fair price with the traders (people who sell things). But how can you pay for your goods? Read on to find out.

AZTEC MARKETS

The best Aztec markets are in Tenochtitlán and the city of Tlatelolco. There are markets every day.

TENOCHTITLÁN MARKET

At dawn the farmers arrive in their canoes. Watch them unload boatloads of maize, fish, and vegetables. By 8 a.m. there will be over 60,000 people!

- Watch the farmers. They weigh out piles of maize (corn).
- Carpenters float logs in from the rainforests. Then they sell them.
- Buy stone, bricks, and tiles. Get them from the **masons'** area. Here men carve stone.
- Visit the bird section. Pick a bird you like. It may be a pigeon, parrot, or owl. Take it home dead or alive!

Colourful fruit, vegetables, and flowers come straight from the rainforest.

WAYS TO PAY

You can pay Aztec traders in different ways. Pay with gold grains for large purchases. People keep grains of gold in a **quill**. This is the long hollow part of a bird's feather. Use cacao beans and copper (metal) bars as small change.

FAIR TRADING

Argue with traders to get the price you want to pay. Don't worry about getting tricked into a bad deal. In large markets, special officers walk around. These are people who check that everyone is selling at fair prices.

Traders show their goods at an Aztec market.

MARKET SQUARES

Tenochtitlán market stretches for many kilometres. It is divided into squares. Different types of goods are sold in each square.

WHAT TO BUY

There's also a craft market. Here you can buy gifts to take home. There are people selling jewellery and clothes. They also sell pots and baskets.

GOLD, PRECIOUS STONES, AND FEATHERS

If you have lots of money, buy some goods made from gold or precious stones. Aztec **craftworkers** make jewellery for the **emperor** (ruler) and noble people. The jewellery is often decorated with patterns and precious stones. Craftworkers also make amazing masks.

Some Aztec masks are made with pieces of stone.

For an unusual present, buy something made from feathers. Feather workers use brightly coloured feathers from birds to make many things. They make headdresses, cloaks, and shields.

MAKING A FEATHER SHIELD

- Women dye the feathers.
- Children mix the glue.
- The men draw a shield design on a piece of cloth.
- They cut the feathers. They stick them onto the cloth.
- The cloth is stretched over a board.
- Feathers and gold thread are added.

AZTEC POTTERY

For cheap gifts, choose pottery. You can buy pottery cooking pots or vases for flowers. You can also buy pottery whistles used by Aztec dancers.

Aztecs used this knife to cut out people's hearts.

CHAPTER 6

KEEPING SAFE AND WELL

You need to be fit and strong to visit the land of the Aztecs. Travellers often suffer from illness. Watch out for attacks by wild animals or Aztec fighters. And try not to be killed as a gift for the gods!

HEALTH CARE

The Aztecs believe that illness is a punishment. The gods send this punishment. But if you become ill you can visit a doctor.

AZTEC DOCTORS

An Aztec doctor may suggest:

- a steam bath for a cold
- a mint drink to help a cough
- pouring liquid rubber into your ear for an earache!

If you are cut, the doctor may sew up the wound with hair.

HEALING

Your Aztec friends may take you to a healer. He may give you drugs. These are made from cactus juice. These make you see things that aren't really there!

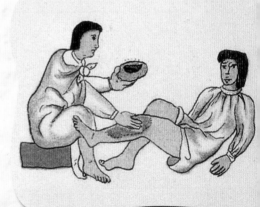

This Aztec doctor is treating someone with an injured leg.

STAYING SAFE

Watch out for **warriors** (fighters). They paint their faces and wear feather headdresses. Aztecs fight with large swords and **javelins**. Javelins are long spears. In battle, the Aztecs sometimes slice off their enemies' ears with their swords!

WILD WARRIORS

The wildest warriors are the jaguar and eagle knights. Jaguar knights dress in suits made from jaguar skins. Eagle knights (like the one in this picture) wear suits of eagle feathers. They wear masks of eagles' heads.

CRIME AND PUNISHMENT

Keep out of trouble! Aztec punishments are very harsh.

Commoners, or ordinary people, cannot wear perfume. They cannot drink hot chocolate. If they do, they are killed immediately.

DON'T LOOK

If you see the **emperor** (ruler) turn away. No one is allowed to look at his face. No one can touch him. If you break these rules, you'll be killed.

The Aztecs built this **temple** for the rain god and Sun god.

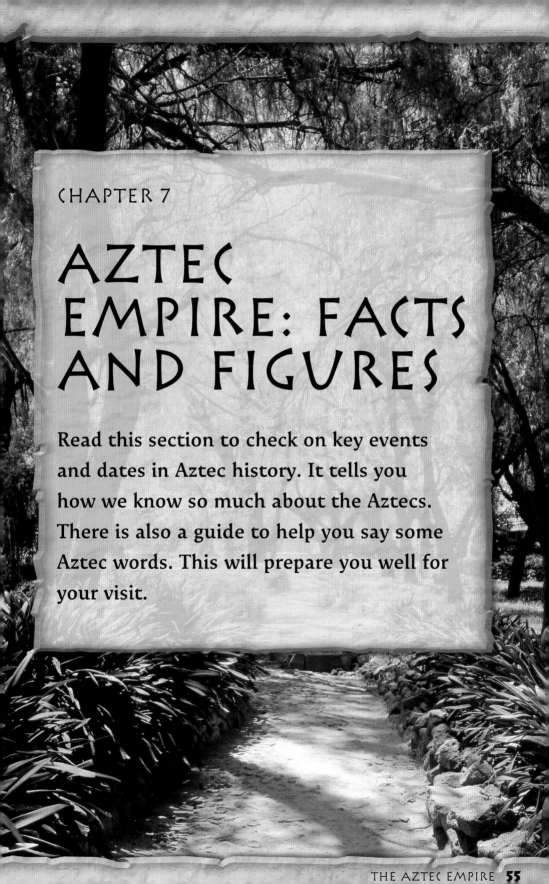

CHAPTER 7

AZTEC EMPIRE: FACTS AND FIGURES

Read this section to check on key events
and dates in Aztec history. It tells you
how we know so much about the Aztecs.
There is also a guide to help you say some
Aztec words. This will prepare you well for
your visit.

HOW WE KNOW ABOUT THE AZTECS

We know about the Aztecs from records of Spanish soldiers. We also know about them from early visitors to their land. **Archaeologists** also help us learn about the Aztecs. Archaeologists dig up statues and objects from the remains of Aztec buildings.

THE SPANISH ARRIVE

In 1517, Spanish soldiers first arrived in Mexico. They were known as conquistadors. Two years later Hernán Cortés led 608 soldiers to the area. He knew about the riches of Tenochtitlán. He was determined to conquer the Aztecs.

A SOLDIER OR A GOD?

About 500 years ago, Cortés and his army arrived in the city of Tenochtitlán. This was 1519. The Aztecs welcomed them with gifts. The Aztecs believed that Cortés was their god Quetzalcoatl. Like their god, Cortés had a pale skin. The Aztec **Emperor** (ruler) Moctezuma II decided to please the god by offering gifts.

A CRUEL MOVE

Moctezuma welcomed Cortés to his city. But Cortés tricked Moctezuma into moving out of his palace. Cortés took control of the Aztec **Empire**. The emperor was now his prisoner.

THE END OF THE AZTEC EMPIRE

Cortés went away to fight another battle. While he was away, the people of Tenochtitlán stood up to their Spanish rulers. Emperor Moctezuma spoke to his angry people. The people attacked him. The emperor died from his wounds.

After this, Cortés left Tenochtitlán. He attacked the city a year later. This time the Aztecs did not fight back. The Spanish conquered the Aztec Empire.

AZTEC HISTORY AT A GLANCE

TIMELINE

(Note: dates are not exact. BC means the years before our modern calendar started. AD is the time of our modern calendar.)

9000 BC	People begin to settle in the Valley of Mexico.
1500 BC	The Mayan **civilization** (society) begins in the Yucatan **peninsula** (land that sticks out into the sea).
AD 250	The Maya build cities in many parts of Mexico.
850	People leave the large Mayan cities.
950	The Toltecs build Tula. They become the most powerful Mexican people.
1100–1200	The Aztecs leave their land in northern Mexico and start to move south.
1168	Different groups destroy Tula. The Toltecs escape to the Yucatan land.
1300	The Aztecs arrive in the Valley of Mexico.
1325	The Aztecs settle beside Lake Texcoco. They begin building the city of Tenochtitlán.
1376	Acamapichtli becomes the first **emperor** (ruler). The Aztecs fight neighbouring tribes.
1428	The Aztecs become the chief powers in the Valley of Mexico.
1458	The Aztecs win large areas of land around the Gulf of Mexico.
1487	The Great **Temple** (religious building) in Tenochtitlán is rebuilt. It is bigger than ever.
1504	A three-year period of **famine** (not enough food) begins. There is disease and earthquake (huge shakes in the Earth).

1519	12 March: Hernán Cortés lands in south-east Mexico. 8 November: Cortés reaches Tenochtitlán. He takes Moctezuma II prisoner.
1520	The Aztecs attack the Spaniards; Moctezuma dies.
1521	13 August: The Spaniards take over the ruins of Tenochtitlán.
1535	Spain takes over control of Mexico.
1540s	Some Aztecs create the "**Codex** Mendoza". This is a picture record of the Aztecs' way of life.
1790	Workmen in Mexico City discover a huge statue of the Aztec goddess Coatlicue.
1791	Workmen uncover the Aztec Stone of the Sun (see page 21).
1900	Aztec remains are found in Mexico City.
1978-1982	People **excavated** (dug up) the remains of the Great Temple of Tenochtitlán.

SPEAK LIKE THE AZTECS

The Aztec people speak Nahuatl (say "nah-wah-tl"). This is a language still spoken in Mexico today. Aztec words and names can seem impossible to **pronounce** (say) at first.

There are a few basic rules to follow. In the end, you should be able to say even the most difficult names.

HOW TO SAY IT

X is like **SH** in "English".

TL sounds like the **TL** in "faintly" (but without the sound of the "y").

CU is like **KW**.

HU is like **W** in "win".

Z is like **S** in "English".

SOME COMMON AZTEC WORDS

Stress the sound which is underlined.

Huitzilopochtli	Weet-see-lo-<u>pocht</u>-lee
Nahuatl (the Aztec language)	Na-<u>wah</u>-tl
Quetzalcoatl (the serpent god, god of creation)	Ket-zal-<u>ko</u>-wat
Tenochtitlán	Te-noch-<u>teet</u>-lan
Teotihuacán	Tay-oh-tee-<u>wah</u>-kan
Texcoco	Tesh-<u>co</u>-co
tlachtli (**sacred** ball game)	tlash-<u>tlee</u>
tlamatini (doctor)	tla-mat-<u>ee</u>-nee
tlatoani (**emperor**)	tla-to-<u>ah</u>-nee

FURTHER READING

BOOKS

Aztec Life, John Clare (Snapping Turtle Guides, 2000)

Excavating the Past: The Aztec Empire, Nicholas Saunders and Tony Allan (Heinemann/Raintree, 2004)

Eyewitness Guide: Aztecs, Elizabeth Baquedano (Dorling Kindersley, 2nd edition, 2006)

WEBSITES

- http://www.mexicolore.co.uk/index.php?one=azt&two=aaa
- http://www.wsu.edu/~dee/CIVAMRCA/AZTECS.HTM
- http://www.guggenheim.org/artscurriculum/lessons/aztec_L8.php
- http://www.ancientmexico.com/content/map/index.html
- http://en.wikipedia.org/wiki/Aztec

GLOSSARY

archaeologist someone who learns about the past by digging up old buildings and objects and examining them

cacao beans beans used to produce chocolate

causeway raised road that connects an island to the mainland

ceremony a formal event or occasion

civilization a society at a particular time in history

clans groups of up to 200 families

codex type of early book, often made from a long strip of folded paper

commoner member of the ordinary people, not a noble or a priest

craftworkers people skilled in a craft such as making jewellery

drought long period of very dry weather

emperor a person who rules a kingdom

empire a large area ruled by an emperor

excavate to dig up

famine serious shortage of food

glyphs pictures that are used to represent an object

incense substance that is burnt to create a sweet smell

javelin pointed metal spear

mainland main part of a country, not an island

mason someone who cuts and carves stone and builds stone buildings

mine dig and remove useful or valuable materials from the ground

peninsula piece of land that sticks out into the sea

pronounce the way to say a word

quill long, hollow central part of a bird's feather

reed tall grass-like plant

sacred place or object that is considered to be holy

sacrifice animal or a human that is killed as a gift for the gods

shrine small temple built in honour of a god

temple building used for religious ceremonies

tribe a group of people

tribute gifts that conquered people have to give to their conquerors, as a form of tax

volcano a mountain that bursts out hot liquid rock and gases

warrior fighter

INDEX